Karl Czerny Piano

Sheet Music Collection 1

C000243259

Copyright ® 2017 Julien Coallier

An Archetype Publishing Production

License Notes

This book is licensed for your personal enjoyment and usage. This book / ebook may not be re-sold or given away to other people unless additional copies are purchased. If you enjoy this book / ebook and have not yet purchased, please buy this book at an authorized book store.

Contents

Czerny Op. 599 No.1

Czerny Op. 599 No.2

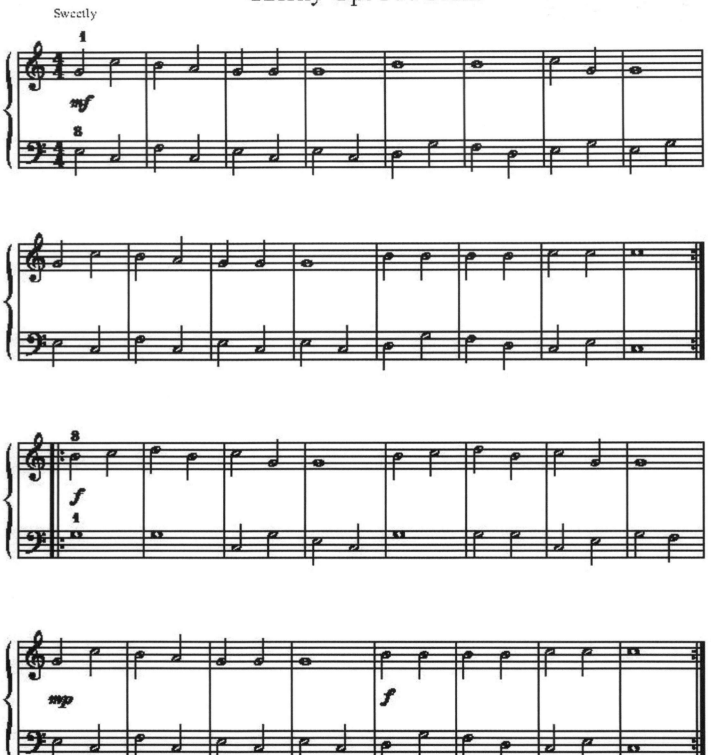

School of Velocity

C. CZERNY. Op.299, Book1.

9

10

Molto Allegro. ($\textit{d}$ = 108)

5.

14

16

Molto Allegro. (♩= 104)

7.

p leggiermente non legato.

cresc.

f

sf

sf

p

pp   dolce.

17

Molto Allegro. (♩ = 104)

8.

Molto Allegro. (♩=108)

9.

p sempre leggiero.

28

legg. staccato.

30

32

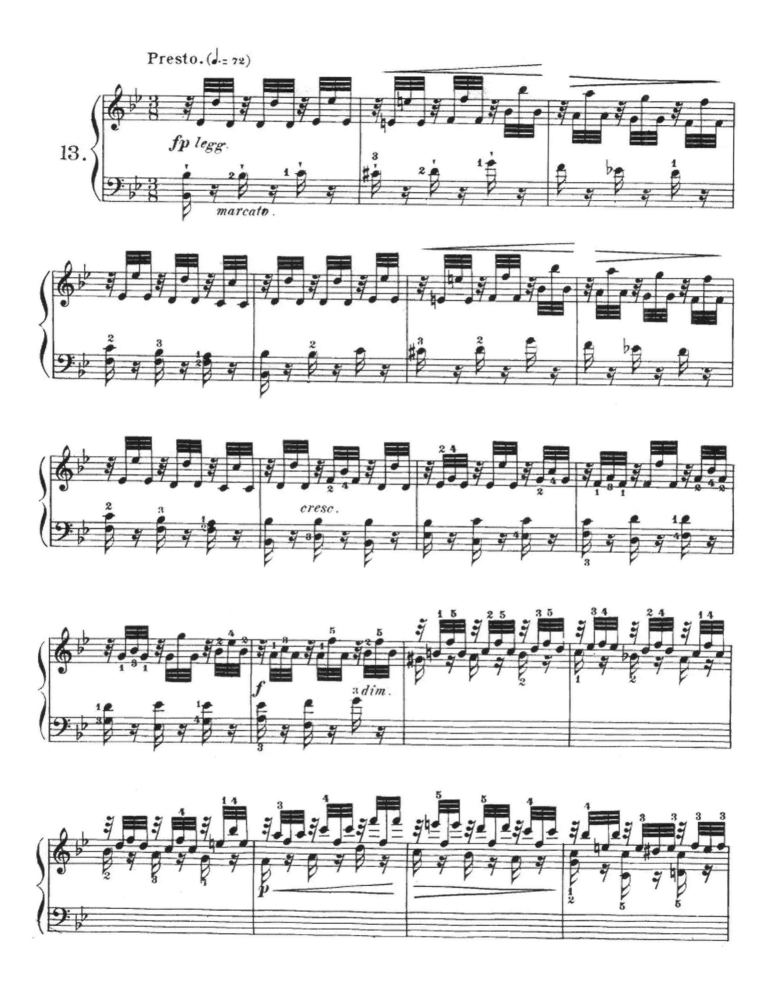

36

Molto vivo e velocissimo. ($\bullet$ = 116)

14.

37

52

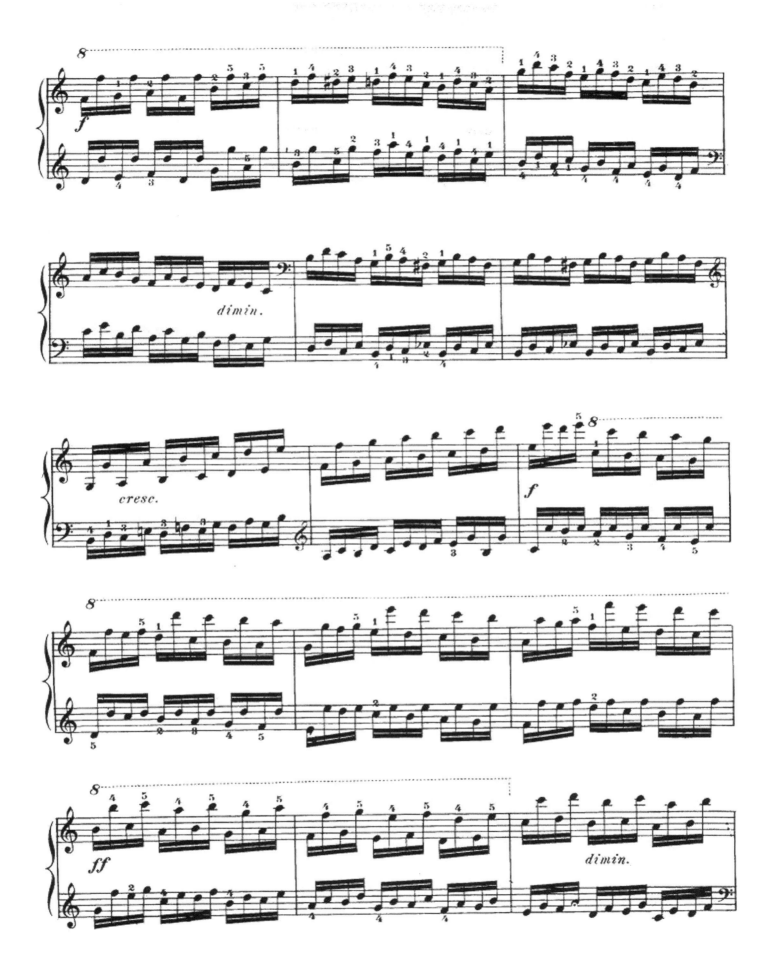

Die Schule der Geläufigkeit.

School of Velocity

C. CZERNY, Op. 299. 3.

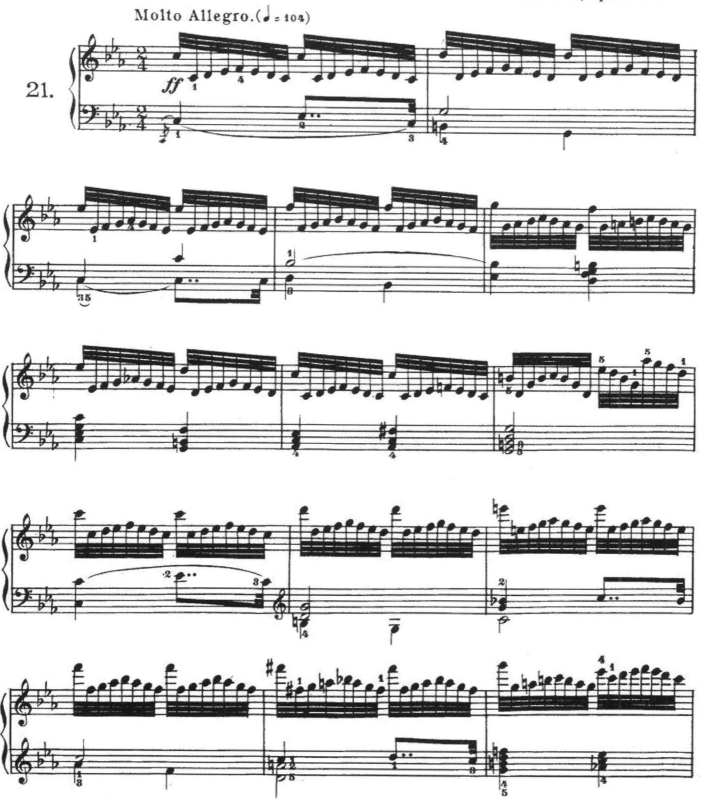

Molto Allegro. ($\bullet$.=63)

23.

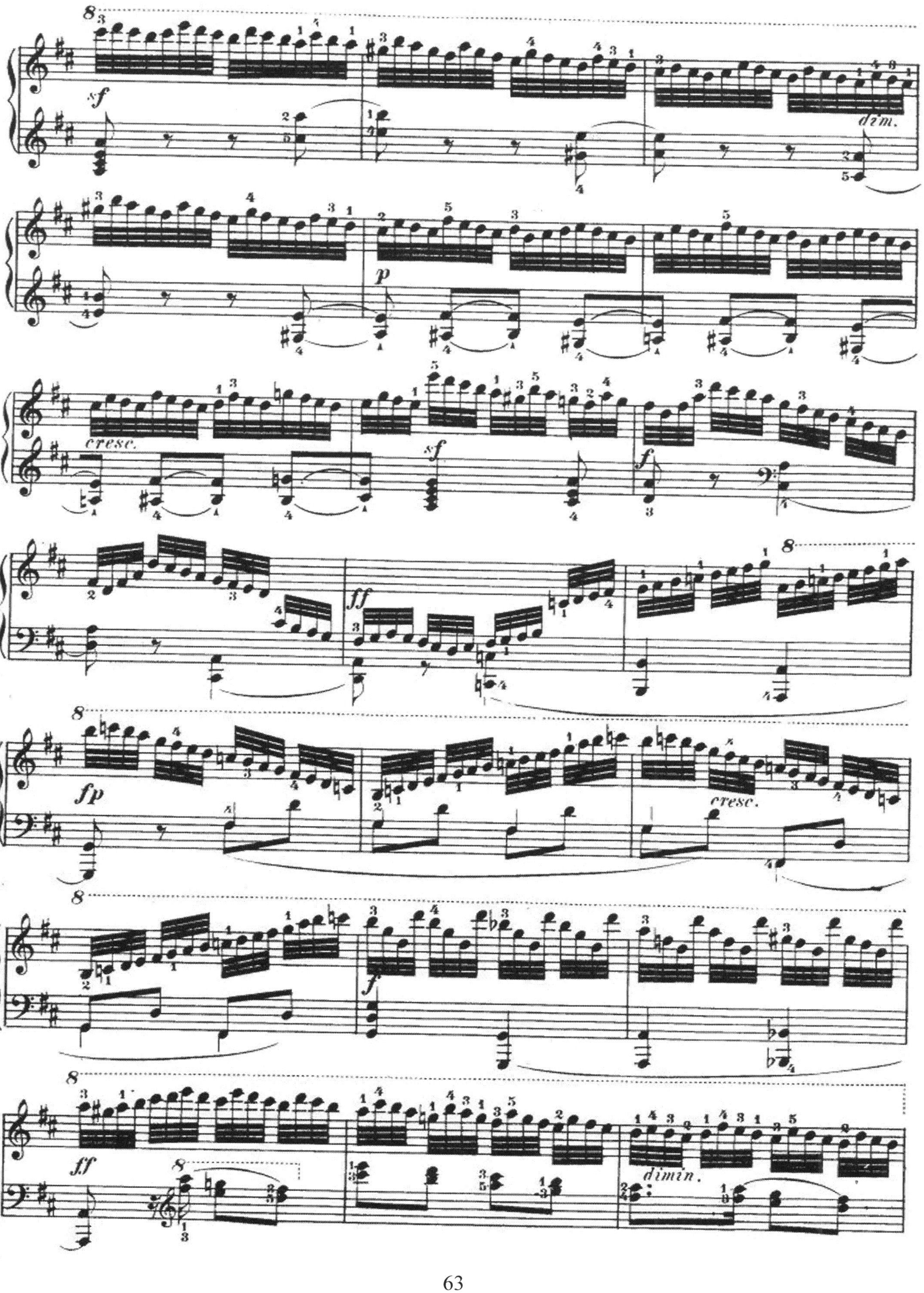
sf
dim.
p
cresc.
sf
f
ff
fp
cresc.
f
ff
dimin.

64

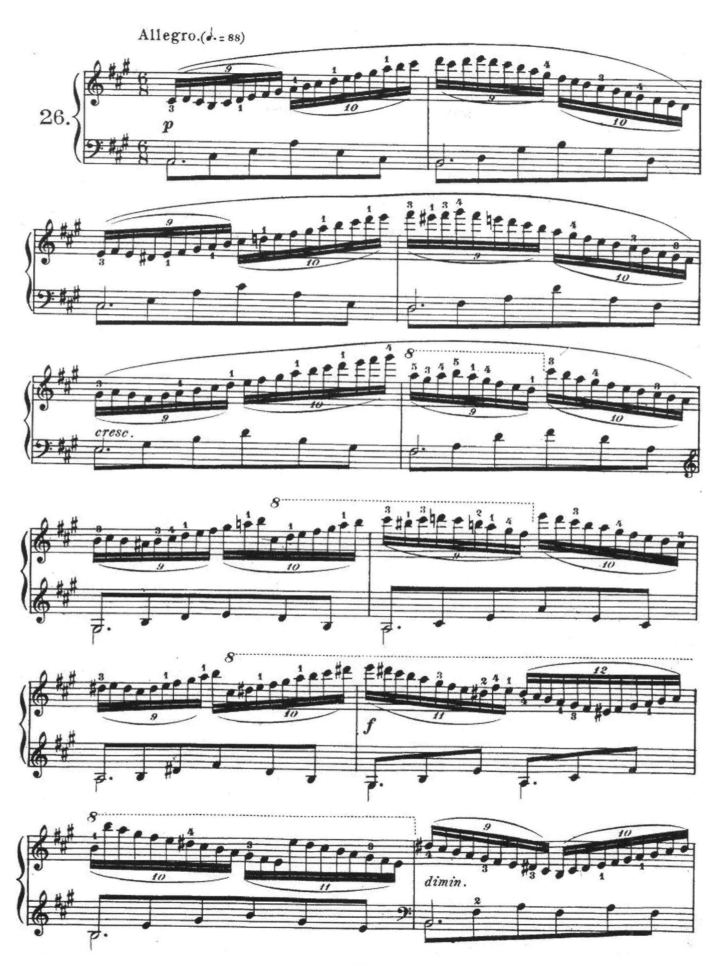

74

School of Velocity

CARL CZERNY. Op.299, 4

Presto volante. (♩ = 100.)

32.

Molto Allegro e giocoso. (♩ = 96.)

37.

95

Molto Allegro, quasi presto. (♩ = 84.)

38.

101

Allegrissimo, quasi presto. ($\bullet$=120)

40.

Printed in Great Britain
by Amazon

60829776R00061